Seaside Maths

About Starters Maths books

STARTERS MATHS have been designed to highlight for young children some everyday situations, to which New Mathematics apply. The topic approach has been used to help the children relate mathematics to the ordinary world around them, by presenting money, number, shape, size and other mathematical ideas in familiar contexts. Children will be able to consolidate their experience in arranging sets, in recognising simple geometric forms and in using other mathematical ideas in ways now widely practised by their teachers. The books also follow the normal school practice of using only metric measures.

The text of each book is simple enough to enable children to read the questions for themselves, as the vocabulary has been carefully controlled to ensure that about 90% of the words used will be familiar to them.

Illustrated by: Geoff Hocking

Written and planned by: Leslie Foster, former Primary School Headmaster and Inspector for Schools, author of *Colour Factor in Action, Play's the Thing, Classes and Counts, Countdown to Christmas, Countdown to Easter* and *Just Look At Computers.*

Managing editor: Su Swallow

Editor: Sandie Oram

Production: Rosemary Bishop

Chairman, teacher panel: F. F. Blackwell, former General Inspector for Schools, London Borough of Croydon, with responsibility for Primary Education.

Teacher panel: Ruth Lucas, Linda Snowden, Mary Todd

ISBN 0 356 04431 9
(cased edition)

ISBN 0 356 11098 2
(limp edition)

© Macdonald and Company (Publishers) Limited 1973
Reprinted 1974 and 1984
Made and printed in Great Britain by Hazell, Watson & Viney Limited
Aylesbury, Buckinghamshire

First published in 1973 by Macdonald and Company (Publishers) Limited
Maxwell House
Worship Street
London EC2A 2EN

Members of BPCC plc

STARTERS
MATHS

Seaside
Maths

Macdonald Educational

These children are at the seaside.
They look down on the sea.
There are fish under the water.
Sea birds fly above their heads.

2

Shells have lovely shapes.
Some are big.
Others are small.
How many shells are stuck to the rocks?

2nd August

Jan	Feb	Mar	Apr	May	Jun
Jul	Aug	Sep	Oct	Nov	Dec

We have holidays in the summer.
What season is it now?
How many months to the summer?

4

The roundabouts go round in a circle.
Use your hands to show
how the other things move.

These creatures live in the sand and sea.
Their bodies are made up of parts.
These are called segments.
Can you count their segments?
6

What has made the pebbles so smooth?
Can you find pebbles
with different shapes and sizes?

The skin diver is swimming in deep water.
The children are paddling
in shallow water.
Is the water in your bath deep or shallow?

8

How many men pull the boat
over the sand?
How many men move the boat
on the rollers?
Which boat is easiest to move?

How many things
fly above the children's heads?
Is the helicopter above the birds?
10

These plants and fish live in the sea.
Look at the shape of the jellyfish.
Can you find a starfish?
How many arms does it have?

DONKEY RIDES 10p

ICES 5p

This boy is paying for a donkey ride.
Other children buy ices and drinks.
Does a donkey ride cost more than an ice?

12

The family try to ring the bell.
The graph shows what happens.
Can you retell the story?

There are many shapes on the beach.
Can you see a ball?
What shape are the flags?
How many cones can you find?

14

Can you find the shapes again?
Can you see a circle?
Find a triangle and a rectangle.

The fat man is being weighed.
His mass is 250 kilograms.
What is your mass?

16

The children are playing on the beach.
They are filling their buckets.
Which do you think will be heavier:
a bucket of pebbles or of water?

17

The children cover their mother with sand.
The net covers part of the beach.
Which covers more: the net or the towel?

18

Do you think it is a hot day?
How do you know?
Is it warmer or cooler in the water?

19

The children have collected shells.
Which box has the least number of shells?
How many shells are in each box?
How many shells altogether?

20

The sea makes patterns in the sand.
What is the girl doing?
Can you see her reflection?
Look at your reflection in a mirror.

21

Find the two boats that are moved
by the wind.
How do the children move their boat?
What moves the liner?

22

At high tide the water covers the beach.
Which picture shows high tide?

23

The children are putting things into water.
Some things float and some sink.
Can you find things which float or sink?
Make a set of things which float.

24

What time did the children
go into the pool?
When did they come out?
How long were they in the water?

The children are dropping balls.
The balls are bouncing.
Find the ball which bounces highest.

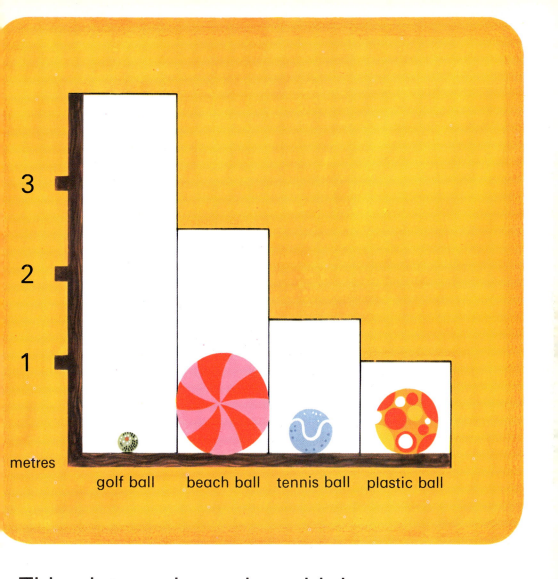

3

2

1

metres

golf ball   beach ball   tennis ball   plastic ball

This picture shows how high
the balls bounced.
How high did the tennis ball bounce?
Which ball bounced $2\frac{1}{2}$ metres?

27

Index

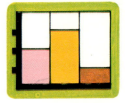

Notes for Parents and Teachers

Here is a brief explanation of the various mathematical points covered in this book, to help the interested adult to explore the topic with children.

Sets and numbers *(pages 7, 12, 18, 24)*

Sets are one of the starting points in modern mathematics. Children sort things into sets *(24)* and use them in various opportunities for counting, with which they can develop an understanding of the processes of addition and subtraction *(7, 18)*, and in the handling of money *(12)*.

Quantities *(pages 2, 4, 5, 16, 17, 20, 25, 26, 27)*

Children learn the terms used in general mathematical comparisons concerned with height, capacity and temperature *(2, 17, 20, 26, 27)*. They also learn the more specific terms for time and the various metric measurements *(4, 16, 25)*.

Space *(pages 2, 3, 5, 6, 8, 10, 11, 14, 15, 19, 21, 23)*

Children learn about simple geometric shapes and discover their names *(3, 11, 14, 15)*. They practise counting on lines *(6)*. They begin to understand concepts like area through practical examples *(19)*. Reflection is used to help them understand more about shape *(21)*. They also study various patterns of movement *(5)* to give them notions of position, distance and direction *(2, 5, 8, 10, 23)*.

Mechanisms *(pages 9, 22, 24)*

Science and mathematics are closely linked studies. Simple mechanisms which illustrate force, such as wheels, rollers and levers, are now included in most maths courses.

Pictorial representation *(pages 13, 27)*

Pictorial representation by graphs of various kinds is one way for children to learn analysis, and it enables them to store information conveniently as well as to interpret it.